Beau

BEAUTIFUL
WILDFLOWERS

A Garland of

American Wildflowers

With 20 Watercolors

by Nanae Ito

♛

HALLMARK EDITIONS

Edited by Bette Bishop

Mildred E. Mathias, Ph.D., Department of Botany,
The University of California at Los Angeles,
Technical Consultant

Illustrations in "Lilies of the Field" reproduced courtesy of the
Linda Hall Library, Kansas City, Missouri.

Copyright © 1968 by Hallmark Cards Inc.,
Kansas City, Missouri. All Rights Reserved.
Printed in the United States of America.
Library of Congress Catalog Card Number: 68-16435.

CONTENTS

INTRODUCTION

"A THING of beauty is a joy forever," wrote the poet John Keats. No statement applies more perfectly to the wildflower—a single plant found by a roadside or a multitude of plants displaying their colors across fields and meadows, in woods and valleys, by streams and lakes, and along mountain ridges. They are Nature's gift to the landscape, and to all who delight in the discovery of floral treasures.

Wildflowers are truly individualists. More than 30,000 different species cover the United States. Selected here are 20 of the most popular and most beautiful, delicately re-created in the evocative watercolors of Nanae Ito.

The panorama of wildflowers is rich not only in beauty, but in legends and tales as well. Many flowers—such as the Thistle, Iris, and Lotus—were sacred to the hearts of certain peoples. And the natural splendor, grace, and charm of wildflowers have always inspired poets and artists.

The descriptive texts that accompany the floral paintings in this book recount the stories and history of each flower. The text was prepared under the guidance of the noted professor of botany at the University of California at Los Angeles, Dr. Mildred E. Mathias. Gray's *Manual of Botany*, the standard work in the field, supplied the scientific names.

Wildflowers, like all of Nature, continue to evolve, and well-known species are even today becoming rare or vanishing entirely. Botanists, at the same time, continue to find new and unusual species to add to those already classified. There will always be new wildflowers to discover.

May *Beautiful Wildflowers* lead you to the floral riches that are our national heritage.

Beautiful wildflowers

BLOODROOT

Sanguinaria canadensis
Poppy Family

SUCH dainty white flowers hardly deserve so blunt a name, but the stems and rootstock of the Bloodroot produce a colorful red-orange dye which American Indians used for war paint and pioneer children used to color their Easter eggs. Early settlers in America believed the plant a remedy for rattlesnake bite and a useful stimulant and tonic. The Bloodroot heralds the approach of spring. Even before the last storm of winter, its exquisite white blossoms often adorn the banks of streams and wooded slopes along the East Coast of the United States and westward to Kansas and Texas.

❧ II ❧

COMMON BLUE VIOLET

Viola papilionacea
violet Family

A FAVORITE native American flower, the Blue Violet grows as far west as Oklahoma. Like other species of Violets, it shows not only the lovely blooms of spring but a seldom-noticed summer flowering too that produces a multitude of self-pollinated seeds. The Violet family is ancient. In Greek mythology, Zeus loved Io, a young maiden, and hid her from Hera's wrath by turning her into a white heifer. The coarse grass Io ate hurt her soft mouth. Zeus changed her tears into food—the sweet-smelling, delicate flower we today call the Violet. In Persia, the Violet made a fine sherbet; in Rome, a perfumed wine. Napoleon's followers chose it as their emblem. It is the state flower of Illinois, New Jersey, Rhode Island, and Wisconsin.

BUTTER-AND-EGGS

Linaria vulgaris
Snapdragon Family

THE bright orange and yellow blossoms of this wildflower account for its unusual name. It is also called "Bacon-and-eggs" and "Bread-and-cheese" for the same reason. It has been called a worse name—Toadflax. In Europe, from which the plant was introduced to America, it was used as a medicine for bubonic plague. Someone along the way misspelled "bubonium" as "bufonium," and "bufo" in Latin means "toad." Butter-and-eggs seems a more appropriate name for a plant that was once the source of a popular beauty lotion. It blossoms from May to October in fields across the United States, its slender stalks sometimes reaching a height of three feet.

BUTTERCUP

Ranunculus acris
Buttercup Family

THE colorful Buttercup glows in meadows throughout the East and Midwest and even into Oregon. Today, as long ago, children love to hold this bright flower under their chins to test their liking for butter! The Buttercup was introduced from Europe, and the English poet Robert Herrick tells a beautiful story of how it acquired its unusual Latin name—*Ranunculus*. Ranunculus was a young Libyan boy noted for his melodious voice and brilliant dress. He wore only green and yellow silk and charmed all who heard his singing. Serenading wood nymphs one day, Ranunculus became so entranced with his own music he expired in ecstasy and turned into the flower that honors his charm and beauty.

14

DUTCHMAN'S BREECHES

Dicentra cucullaria
Bleeding-Heart Family

THE dainty Dutchman's Breeches is the delight of children. Its tiny white pantaloons are suspended from slightly arching stalks so that the touch of yellow—the belt—hangs down and the pointed ends project upward. The generic name describes these "pants": *Dicentra*, derived from a Greek word meaning "two-spurred." The little Dutchmen prefer rocky ledges and rich woods, where, in April, they put forth almost heart-shaped blossoms framed with fernlike leaves. They are found in New England, in parts of the Midwest, and as far west as Washington and Oregon. Attempts to cultivate the plant in new locations have failed, unfortunately, and these delicate flowers are becoming scarce even in areas where they once flourished.

FRINGED GENTIAN

Gentiana crinita
Gentian Family

PERHAPS the best description of this delightful flower comes from Henry David Thoreau: "Such a dark blue! surpassing that of a male bluebird's back!" The Fringed Gentian, floral emblem of autumn, grew in profusion in the kingdom of King Gentius of Illyria in eastern Europe and was named in his honor. It is found in wet woods and meadows of the eastern United States. In Hungarian folklore, the plant's discovery is attributed to King Ladislas. During a plague epidemic, in desperation, he shot an arrow into the air, praying that the Lord would direct it to a curative plant. The arrow lodged in the root of a Gentian, which miraculously cured his people.

❧ VII ❧

GOLDENROD

Solidago canadensis
Daisy Family

MORE than one hundred species of Goldenrod ornament roadsides and meadows throughout the United States in late summer and early autumn. An old European myth describes the plant's creation. Tired from her journey through the woods, an elderly woman asked several trees for one of their branches to use as a staff. All refused, but a stick lying on the ground said, "I am old and ugly, but perhaps strong enough to help you." Out of the woods, the woman changed into a beautiful fairy and promised the stick anything it desired. "To be loved by children," it replied. She planted it, scattered fairy gold over it, and said, "Hereafter you shall be known as Goldenrod, and children shall love you." It is the state flower of Kentucky and Nebraska.

JACK-IN-THE-PULPIT

Arisaema triphyllum
Calla Family

THE shy Jack-in-the-Pulpit is easily overlooked. Its quiet green does not stand out from the shady woods where it normally grows. It is an early sign of spring, flowering from April to June. The flowers of the Calla family were known several hundred years before Christ; Aristotle records the belief that this plant restores life to bears after their winter hibernation. The Jack-in-the-Pulpit is a legendary Crucifixion flower. The purple veins marked on its leafy "pulpit" are said to be the marks of drops of blood received from the Cross. In America, its bright red berries were an Indian delicacy, and its root, nutritious when thoroughly boiled, gave it the name "Indian Turnip."

LARGE BLUE FLAG

Iris versicolor
Iris Family

In late spring, this lovely flower forms a blue mantle over fields and marshes in New England and westward to Minnesota. It is one of a striking genus of wildflowers — Iris — named for the Greek goddess of the rainbow. She was said to be the fleet-footed messenger of Zeus and Hera, and the rainbow formed the bridge she used to cross from heaven to earth. The Iris plant is believed to be the original source of the famous fleur-de-lis — the heraldic emblem associated with the royal coat of arms of France, which dates from the 12th century. If so, "fleur-de-lis" is a misnomer, since it means "flower of the lily."

LILY-OF-THE-VALLEY

Convallaria majalis
Lily Family

THE Lily-of-the-Valley's creation is the subject of an old English legend. St. Leonard, the legend goes, encountered the terrible dragon, Sin, and for three days struggled against it. On the fourth morning, the dragon could fight no more. It crawled away, leaving St. Leonard victorious but wounded. And wherever the good man's blood had fallen Lilies-of-the-Valley sprang up. People believed they could trace the battle by the tiny bell-like flowers growing in the woods, and if they listened carefully, they would hear the victory chimes. This delightful flower—a garden plant introduced from Europe —adds a fairyland look to wooded areas when it puts forth its miniature bell-blossoms in May and June.

PAINTED CUP

Castilleja coccinea
Snapdragon Family

MOTHER Nature used her most brilliant pigments to paint this striking plant. The flowers themselves are inconspicuous, their yellow-green points almost concealed by the fiery scarlet bracts which are really modified leaves. Various species of Painted Cup color the summer landscape across the United States. The flower is also called Indian Paint Brush, and is known by that name as the state flower of Wyoming. Henry David Thoreau wrote of it: "It is a splendid show of brilliant scarlet.... I do not like the name. It does not remind me of a cup, rather of a flame when it first appears. It might be called Flame-Flower, or Scarlet Tip...."

28

❧ XII ❧

PASQUEFLOWER

Anemone patens
Buttercup Family

SOMETIMES known as the Easter Flower or The Flower of the Resurrection, the Pasqueflower ranks among the lovelier species of Anemone. It was listed as one of the plants used to dye Easter eggs for the Easter Court Festival of King Edward I. The flower produces a brilliant green dye. The Greek myth of Zephyr and Anemone is associated with this genus of flowers. The nymph Anemone died of a broken heart and was changed by Venus into a flower, and Zephyr, the wind god, fanned her each day with his wings. The Pasqueflower, also called Prairie Smoke, is the state flower of South Dakota. It appears in springtime in the fields of the Midwest and as far north as Washington.

SHOWY LADY'S SLIPPER

Cypripedium reginae
Orchid Famiy

THE unusual and charming Showy Lady's Slipper is one of America's largest Orchids. It grows in New England and south and west to Georgia and Missouri, and attains its most magnificent appearance in limestone soil. The botanical name of this genus of plants refers to the slipper of Aphrodite, the goddess of love and beauty. *Cypripedium reginae* means "lady's slipper of the queen." The lovely Lady's Slipper is associated with Christian legend as well. Many people believe that flowers with the name "Lady" were originally dedicated to Mary, Mother of Jesus.

SPIDERWORT

Tradescantia virginiana
Dayflower Family

THE deep blue or purple flowers of the Spider-wort grow in great numbers along roadsides and meadows in late spring and throughout the summer, from Maine to Tennessee and Missouri. This showy flower acquired its name because its narrow grass-shaped leaves spread out spider-like around its blossom. The Spiderwort belongs to the genus *Tradescantia*, a name which honors John Tradescant, gardener to Charles I, King of England. Tradescant was a botanical explorer and the founder of the Museum of Natural History at Lambeth, London, England. The Spiderwort is most lovely in the morning, when its three brilliant petals open wide to display spectacular golden anthers.

COMMON SUNFLOWER

Helianthus annuus
Daisy Family

THE Sunflower is one of several plants with the unique ability to direct its full face to the sun, following that light source across the sky each day. When Spanish explorers reached Peru in 1532, they found the Inca Indians worshipping the Sunflower as a living symbol of their sun god. The Plains Indians of North America also included it in their religious rites. A practical wildflower, its seeds produce oil used to make margarine and artists' paints. The Chinese manufacture a beautiful cloth of fibers derived from its stem. The yellow and brown "flower of the sun" grows along roadsides and in meadows in almost all parts of the United States, and is the state flower of Kansas.

⚜ XVI ⚜

SWAMP THISTLE

Cirsium muticum
Daisy Family

THE Thistle was a favorite of Thor, the Norse god of thunder, and was once called the "lightning plant." Those who wore it were thought to be protected from harm. The prickly flower is the National Emblem of Scotland, an honor which dates back to the Danish Wars. The Danes took off their boots to surprise a Scottish camp at night. All went well until a soldier stepped on a thistle. His cry of pain awakened the Scots. They defeated the invaders and made the "guardian thistle" their national floral symbol. The hollow stems of the Swamp Thistle sometimes reach a height of ten feet. Blooms appear from July to September in moist woods and swamps throughout New England, southward to Maryland and inland as far as Louisiana.

✒ XVII ✒

SWEET-BRIER ROSE

Rosa eglanteria
Rose Family

THE rose is the oldest and most famous flower in the world. It has been a symbol of love and an inspiration to poets from the time of Homer. In painting, in religion, in heraldry and in the gardens of the great the rose has held a prominent place. The Sweet-Brier is England's Eglantine, celebrated by Shakespeare and brought to America by British settlers to remind them of home. It grows now in many parts of the United States, flowering from mid-May to July, a large shrub rose so thorny it makes a hedge as impassable as barbed wire. After the plant flowers, large hips form and ripen to a bright orange, making it beautiful in fall and winter as well.

WILD COLUMBINE

Aquilegia canadensis
Buttercup Family

THE graceful, vase-like shape of the Columbine has for centuries provided artists with a model of perfect form. The flower appears as part of the illuminated border of a hand-lettered manuscript dating from the late 15th century. An association was once formed to make the Columbine the national floral emblem of the United States. The flower's common name suggests Columbia, a popular patriotic name for America, and the botanical name is similar to the eagle's. The association did not accomplish its purpose, but Colorado later adopted the Columbine as its state flower. Sometimes called Rock Bells, Columbine may be found throughout the United States, growing usually on rocky wooded ledges.

WOOD LILY

Lilium philadelphicum
Lily Family

THE Wood Lily is primarily an Eastern flower, although varieties of it may be found as far west as New Mexico. A familiar legend gives the lily a prominent place in the Passion of Christ. Before the Crucifixion, the legend goes, all lilies were white. But Christ looked upon a lily in the Garden of Gethsemane, and so overcome with shame at her unworthiness was the flower that she blushed and bowed her head. Red lilies appeared then, and ever after, and only a few species hold their heads erect when fully formed. The Wood Lily's fragile loveliness enhances the beauty of the open woods, clearings, and dry thickets that are its home.

WOOD-VETCH

Vicia caroliniana
Bean Family

THE slender, vine-like Wood-Vetch is one of America's most common wildflowers. Although in appearance a small plant, it often attains a height of five or six feet, supporting itself by means of its long trailing tendrils. Some species of vetch can be used as fertilizer to restore worn-out soil. There is a bacterium in the roots of these plants which takes nitrogen from the air to form fertile nitrates. The Wood-Vetch grows in profusion along riverbanks and roadsides and in wooded areas in most parts of the country except the western United States. It flowers from April to June, creating the illusion of a mauve carpet spread across the ground.

LILIES OF THE FIELD

By Richard Rhodes

WE cherish flowers for their beauty. Unknowingly, perhaps we also cherish them because we owe them our first debt—the debt of life itself. The first wildflowers, flowering plants, were the ancient ancestors of the lovely things in this book, and they held the chain of evolution together.

There was a time before flowers, but no one remembers it. Man could not be before flowers were. "The weight of a petal . . . changed the world and made it ours," writes the eloquent naturalist Loren Eiseley.

Flowers exploded from a monotonous world of lizards and pines. Before flowers and their magical seeds, the best that nature had produced among animals were slow-brained reptiles and fish, and pollen-propagated ferns and trees among plants. Everything was low-energy: a world of slow motion, not of action; a world of green, not of rainbow colors.

And man had not appeared. His evolution awaited the evolution of the flowers. The

49

largest mammals alive were no larger than the squirrels that today climb our trees. Birds were yet to come. Flapping lizards with leather wings commanded the skies.

Then, suddenly, within a scant million years —overnight when measured on the scale of the earth's long age—the flowers came and the earth quickened. The flowers came in vast variety, with a single purpose: to create at their withering a fully fertilized seed unlike the primitive seeds and scattered pollens of the past. This seed was in fact a miniature plant packed within a casing of high-energy food. It was a seed that could be carried by the wind or on the fur of beasts or in the stomachs of birds. It could take root farther and farther away from the brothy swamps, and sustain the tiny plant within its casing until it grew up to meet the sun.

The seed that fed itself also fed the mammals and the birds. Thus, they could give up exhausting grazing. They could face the cold without sluggishness. They could develop a working brain and furnace its intense activity.

Soon grasses swayed where only rock had slept before. Flowers argued with crevices in the sides of mountains and outfought trees for room in forest clearings. The giants gave way. The dinosaurs went to sleep in beds of limestone.

Morbus articularis.

Illustrations from the earliest known American herbal,
an Aztec medical text dated 1552, now in the
Vatican Library.

The tall ferns left the imprint of their leaves in
deep-buried coal. The redwoods endured as
silent outcasts in a compound of California hills.
Quick things, lithe things—flowers, mammals,

insects, and birds—occupied the continents and brightened them as never before.

And brighten the continents still. North America alone, botanists estimate, grows more than 30,000 varieties of wildflowers. Compare this number to the number of grains, the number of trees, the number of shrubs and vines, the number of animals. Only the insects are more various and prolific, and what would become of them without the flowers?

A Perfectly Adjusted Creation

What is a wildflower? It is a flowering plant that grows without cultivation—like the Wood Lily, the Jack-in-the-Pulpit, the Goldenrod. All flowering plants were once wild; most still are. We have cultivated the most ambitious among them, coaxed and distorted them into specialized forms—fragrant roses, nourishing potatoes, juicy strawberries. Old friends now, they feed us, perfume our walks, and decorate our tables. Meanwhile, their multitudinous relatives, unwilling to labor in employment and be consumed, continue to color the riverbanks and surprise sleepy rabbits on the forest floor.

The wildflower is a perfectly adjusted creation. It is small and sparse enough to survive the grazings of animals, adaptable enough to proliferate in outlandish climates. It thrives on mountain tops, under deep snows, in swamps and valleys, in the cracks of sidewalks and vacant yards—wherever it finds a little soil and water.

You can almost always find a sprig of wild mint nestled against the footings of a house. Who has not blamed the wild dandelion which as a child he adored? Wildflowers are everywhere. They have become such familiar companions we seldom notice them at all unless they trouble us. Is it possible they are older than we? It is. Could they have helped us and our animals rise up from the swamps? They did.

We owe wildflowers a debt, but they set up no clamor for its repayment. They are various, quiet, beautiful, and serene. They are the lilies of the field we were asked to consider. They toil not, neither do they spin. In all his glory, not even Solomon was arrayed like one of these.

Like all plants, wildflowers are classified scientifically by their similarities to one another. The broadest category of classification is the Family. Within the Family appear several *genera* (the plural of *genus*). Within each *genus* appear several species. A flower's scientific name is made up of its *genus*—the name which appears first—and its species. A Family, a *genus*, and a species. The system works without too much confusion, and botanists in every part of the world can use it. The Lily Family, for example, includes the *genera* called *Veratrum*, *Camassia*, and *Lilium*. The *genus* Lilium includes a number of species such as *canadense* (Canada Lily) and *superbum* (Turk's Cap Lily). Which brings us to the flower's common name. The common name is the name we amateurs assign to the flowers out of affection or in fun. It's often a local name, which means we identify wildflowers differently in different parts of the country. One region's Pasqueflower is another's Prairie Smoke; one region's charming Jack-in-the-Pulpit is another's derisive Indian Turnip.

Wildflowers in America

Wildflowers, like gold and land, attracted explorers to the New World. The harsh Spanish who conquered the high civilizations of South America sought Aztec gold, but they also discovered, and came to respect, Aztec medicine. The earliest-known American book of wildflowers is an Aztec herbal translated into Latin in 1552 by an Indian convert. Some of its medical principles still hold good today.

Indian medicine attracted settlers to North America as well. Sassafras was a popular blood tonic and soup thickener among American Indians. It excited Europe for its supposed medicinal properties as penicillin would later excite the world. The bark commanded the highest prices on the Continent. Sassafras-collecting could assure a colony's income. It was probably no accident that one of the first English settlements in America, at Jamestown, Va., was located in the best sassafras country in the region.

Europe also became excited over the floral riches of the New World, partly because the 18th century was a century of elaborate gardens on country estates. The search for medicines and spices gave way to the search for colorful new flowers and trees. Collectors braved great hardship to explore a land where they could be the first men in the world to find and return to Europe a new tree, a new flower, a new kind of fruit. No astronaut could feel better about walking on the moon than the early collectors did about walking on virgin American soil—and there are no wildflowers to discover on the airless, dusty moon.

More practical nations sought not only flowers but new sources of food. The science of botany came into its own in 1837 when the Swedish scholar Carl Linnaeus published his brilliant system of plant classification, the system still used today. Sweden sent to America one of her best young botanists, Peter Kolm, to find new grasses and vegetables to feed a nation periodically and terribly riven by famine.

Linnaeus's system helped accelerate the explorations. Since the Middle Ages, Europe had studied its herbals, books of herbs and wildflowers that clumsily categorized plants and listed their culinary and medicinal uses. Now, with the precise guidelines Linnaeus had developed, botanists searched for new species of plants to expand the horizons of agriculture and natural science.

The King's Botanist

Most of the discoverers came from England, but one of the first and best was an American settler, a self-taught Pennsylvania Quaker farmer named John Bartram. After years of thrifty but routine farming, Bartram discovered in himself a love of wildflowers that led him to explore much of eastern America and to develop a famous garden on his farm. He communicated his discoveries to England, and to his surprise was appointed the King's Botanist in the New World. Most of the collectors who visited America stopped at Bartram's garden to converse and admire.

A new, more scientific flower book began to

Title page of an elegant herbal
published at London in 1597.

appear, replacing the old herbals. Mark Catesby, a Londoner, produced one of the earliest, and the first illustrated in color. He personally financed his initial trip to America, but a decade later, at 39, he was able to return at the expense of wealthy collectors who valued his knowledge and his energetic urge to explore the new continent. He brought back seeds and pressings, and ultimately produced two beautiful volumes describing American flowers and animals, *The Natural History of Carolina, Florida, and the Bahama Islands.* Short on funds, he engraved and hand-colored the first edition himself.

Hostile Indians and a hostile environment made plant-collecting in the New World the work of only the most courageous of explorers. David Douglas wandered the Pacific Northwest and brought the Douglas fir back to civilization. His hardships were typical of those many explorers encountered. "If a change does not take place," he wrote in his journal after days of continuous rain, "I will shortly be consigned to the tomb." The change came, he found the pines and flowers he was seeking, and then he and his party of trappers *walked* from Vancouver to Hudson Bay, across most of Canada.

Douglas's contribution to the treasury of wildflowers was immense. He discovered in America more kinds of plants than any other man of his time had found, and he sent them back to the civilized world by means of seeds which gar-

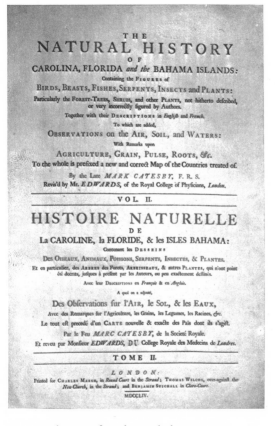

Title page of Mark Catesby's pioneering *Natural History*, first published in 1746.

deners could nurture. Years later, the descendants of his seeds returned to America by way of commercial flower companies as cultivated plants that brightened American gardens. Virginia clematis, the Mariposa lily, blue flax, evening primrose, the California poppy, the annual sunflower, phlox, Lewisia, and more, were Douglas's legacy.

'One Sweet Bee-Garden'

Today, American wildflowers, like the American frontier, have retreated before the cities and farms of men. We have gained, but we have also lost. What would we give now—or fifty years from now—to see what John Muir once saw in California? "When California was wild," he wrote as late as 1911, "it was one sweet bee-garden throughout its entire length. . . . Zones of polleny forests, zones of flowery chaparral, stream tangles of rubus and wild rose, sheets of golden compositae, beds of violets, beds of mint, beds of bryanthus and clover, and so on, certain species blooming somewhere all the year round. . . . The Great Central Plain of California, during the months of March, April, and May, was one smooth, continuous bed of honey bloom, so marvelously rich that, in walking from one end of it to the other, a distance of more than four hundred miles, your foot would press about a hundred flowers at every step."

Those halcyon days are gone forever, but wildflowers can still be found in abundance across the American landscape. Some prefer a damp climate, others a dry. Some are tiny and pale, others tall and showy, others fragile, others strong. Some bloom in springtime, others in summer, others in fall. A few hardy types brave the winter. Their shadings, patterns, and textures approach infinite variety.

Like people, some have been geniuses, devising striking colors and subtle medicines. Some have been beautiful, inspiring poets and painters to art. Some are frighteningly plain. A few are murderous. Most are benign, enjoyable, and excellent company on a pleasant day.

Try your backyard. The odds are good you'll find at least one species right there.

Set at the Castle Press in Bembo, a Venetian face
first cut in 1495 for the printer Aldus Manutius Romanus
and named by him in honor of the humanist poet
(later Cardinal) Pietro Bembo.
Printed on Hallmark Eggshell Book paper.
Designed by Harald Peter.